	DATE DUE		

THE U.S. AUTO INDUSTRY

American Carmakers and the Economic Crisis

Jeri Freedman

ROSEN
PUBLISHING®

New York

Published in 2011 by The Rosen Publishing Group, Inc.
29 East 21st Street, New York, NY 10010

Copyright © 2011 by The Rosen Publishing Group, Inc.

First Edition

Library of Congress Cataloging-in-Publication Data

Freedman, Jeri.
The U.S. auto industry : American carmakers and the economic crisis / Jeri Freedman.
    p. cm. — (In the news)
Includes bibliographical references and index.
ISBN 978-1-4358-9448-8 (library binding) —
ISBN 978-1-4488-1680-4 (pbk.) —
ISBN 978-1-4488-1688-0 (6-pack)
1. Automobile industry and trade—United States—Juvenile literature.
2. Financial crises—Government policy—United States—Juvenile litera-ture. 3. Business failures—Economic aspects—United States—Juvenile literature. 4. United States—Economic conditions—2009—Juvenile liter-ature. I. Title. II. Title: US auto industry.
HD9710.U52F735 2011
338.4'76292220973—dc22

                                                    2009049921

Manufactured in the United States of America

CPSIA Compliance Information: Batch #S10YA: For further information, contact Rosen Publishing, New York, New York, at 1-800-237-9932.

On the cover: Clockwise from top left: A member of the United Auto Workers union is on strike outside of a manufacturing plant in Janesville, Wisconsin, in 2007; Chrysler unveils its ecoVoyager luxury electric car in 2008; GM headquarters in Detroit, Michigan.

contents

Upheaval in the Auto Industry

The U.S. economy suffered a great blow in 2008. The housing market collapsed, the stock market crashed, and the banking industry suffered huge financial losses. Some of the largest banks had to be bailed out with loans from the U.S. government. Banks stopped granting loans to businesses and individuals, afraid they might not be repaid. It was the worst financial crisis the United States had faced since the Great Depression (1929–1939).

The three major U.S. auto companies—Chrysler, Ford, and General Motors (GM)—saw their sales drop dramatically. According to accounting industry organization Grant Thornton, in the first six months of 2009, vehicle sales dropped 35 percent. Chrysler and GM were hit the hardest. According to the December 1, 2009, issue of the *Wall Street Journal*, in 2009 GM's share of the U.S. automotive market dropped to 19.7 percent, from 22.2 percent a year earlier, and Chrysler's market share fell to 9 percent, from 11 percent a year earlier. Although Ford's sales also dropped from the previous year, it picked up customers from its harder hit competitors and posted a small gain in market share, rising to 15.3 percent, up from 14.4 percent a year earlier.

The immediate cause of the decline of the American automotive industry was the economic downturn that sent the United States into a recession. But the origins of the problems faced by these car manufacturers go back much farther. Ultimately, the decline of the American auto industry was the result of decades of poor decisions made by industry management.

Chrysler and General Motors have closed hundreds of car dealerships as part of their cost-cutting measures. This Chicago Chrysler dealership went out of business in 2009.

Deep-Rooted Problems

Some of the problems of the U.S. auto industry are extremely deep-rooted. The industry has a corporate structure based on business conditions that existed decades ago. At that time, the auto industry made a number of very generous deals with union workers. For instance, union workers in the auto industry received health care for life. Even after they retired, these workers still received health care that was paid for by the company. This reflects how business was done for much of the twentieth century, and it was one of the reasons why a job in the auto industry was so desirable. However, companies today rarely offer such extensive benefits to their workers. Car companies in some other countries, such as Japan, were able to implement less expensive arrangements with their workforce because they entered the market decades later.

American auto industry management made certain assumptions that ended up harming the industry. For example, throughout the twentieth and twenty-first centuries, U.S. manufacturers maintained an emphasis on making large cars and trucks. They believed this was what most American consumers wanted. They did not focus on making small, inexpensive, fuel-efficient cars, as they believed that only people without much money would be attracted to these vehicles. This attitude allowed Japanese automakers to dominate the small car market. By 2008, the small car market represented 18 percent of all vehicle sales in the United States—and that percentage is still growing. Many of the small cars that were produced by U.S. carmakers were less reliable than the Japanese cars. As a result, Japanese companies ultimately took control of a large segment of the

U.S. auto market that had once belonged only to Chrysler, Ford, and GM.

The economic recession of 2008 didn't only affect American car companies. It affected foreign car companies as well. However, foreign car companies were generally in a better position to weather the downturn in auto sales. Many of them had less debt, or more cash, than their U.S. counterparts. This enabled them to withstand a drop in revenue and still have enough money to cover their costs. Some Japanese companies, such as Toyota and Honda, have strong reputations for making quality vehicles. They are also at the forefront of building new hybrid cars, which use less gasoline. The effects of the downturn in auto sales resulted in Toyota selling more cars than GM for the first time in 2009.

The Big Three

Today, the United States is home to three domestic car companies: Chrysler, Ford, and GM. Together, these companies are often referred to as the "Big Three." The U.S. car market is valued at more than $382 billion.

In an article on Time.com, "Is General Motors Worth Saving?," Bill Saporito provides the following figures on the influence of the Big Three U.S. automakers. The figures come from a report by the Center for Automotive

Research (CAR). According to CAR, Chrysler, Ford, and GM directly employ about 240,000 people. Another 974,000 people are employed by companies that supply parts and other goods to the Big Three. "Together," says CAR, "these 1.2 million workers spend enough to keep 1.7 million more people employed. That gets you to 2.9 million jobs tied to Detroit."

The auto industry has a vast influence on the American economy. For this reason, the federal government did not want to see the major automotive manufacturers fail. If they went out of business, millions of people would be unemployed, and a large number of other businesses would fail.

Bailing Out the Automakers

The government took steps to stop the auto industry from completely collapsing. At first, it provided loans to GM and Chrysler, which allowed them to keep operating. When the companies still failed, the government carefully orchestrated a streamlined bankruptcy process. This bankruptcy process would allow the auto companies to reorganize and resume operations as quickly as possible.

Not everyone agreed that the government should have intervened to keep these companies afloat. Some people felt the auto companies were in trouble because of bad decisions they had made in the past. These people felt the companies should suffer the consequences of their actions. Others believed in an economic theory called free-market capitalism. According to this theory, the economy works best without government intervention. Badly run companies fail and other, better-run companies replace them. In this way, the market theoretically regulates itself. Many people who had lost jobs in other industries resented that the government helped the automakers while letting other companies fail. To these people, it appeared

Seen here are *(left to right)* UAW president Ron Gettelfinger, Ford CEO Alan Mulally, and Chrysler CEO Robert Nardelli. They are addressing a U.S. Senate hearing on the auto industry on November 18, 2009.

that the government didn't consider companies in other industries important enough to bail out.

On the other side of the argument were many people who believed that not bailing out the auto industry would have disastrous consequences. They thought it could result in massive unemployment in the United States, which could lead to a long economic depression with drastic consequences for the U.S. economy. According to this argument, if too many people were

out of work and not able to buy goods, U.S. companies' sales would decline. As a consequence, these companies would have to lay off their workers. These workers then would not have enough money to buy goods. This process would lead to a downward spiral, and the U.S. economy would just keep getting worse.

The General Motors world headquarters building is located on Jefferson Avenue in Detroit, Michigan. It is considered a Detroit landmark.

The End of Prosperity

It's tempting to think of the U.S. auto industry as nothing more than a collection of giant, faceless corporations. However, these corporations employed millions of workers. The collapse of the industry had an immediate and very serious effect on these workers.

This is especially true in the state of Michigan and the city of Detroit, Michigan, in particular. Detroit was a major manufacturing center for the Big Three automakers, as well as many of their suppliers. Many people living in Detroit were dependent on the automotive industry. The factories there provided people with well-paying

Community activists protest the eviction of a man from his home in Detroit.

jobs that came with good benefits. People had become affluent over the past several decades working in the auto industry. Then more and more of these people began to be laid off. Some laid-off workers found that they no longer had enough money to keep their homes.

Even with the attempts of the federal government to assist automakers, thousands of people still lost their jobs. Of these people, many have had difficulty finding other work. In addition, local companies that depend on these employees for business, such as shops and restaurants, have seen their sales fall off. This threatens these businesses' ability to survive.

As people's unemployment benefits ran out, many could no longer pay the mortgages on their homes. Unpaid mortgages resulted in foreclosure, or the bank taking over the house. As the number of foreclosed homes rose, house prices fell. Soon there were many houses for sale on the market, which made it difficult for people in financial trouble to sell their homes. This, in turn, led to more foreclosures.

The collapse of the auto industry affected state governments as well. The car companies, as well as the companies that supplied them, provided a great deal of tax revenue. As the companies collapsed, they did not provide as much tax revenue. This left the state government with less funds to spend on services for citizens.

The Root of the Problem

2

The present fate of U.S. auto manufacturers is deeply tied to their structure, their philosophy, and the decisions they have made, especially those concerning the types of cars that they make. This chapter provides a historical perspective on how Chrysler, Ford, and GM got where they are today.

History of the Big Three Automakers

In 1903, Henry Ford founded the Ford Motor Company in Dearborn, Michigan. Just ten years later, in 1913, Ford became the first company to engage in mass production by creating and using the first moving assembly line. The company used the assembly line to produce its cars quickly to meet growing demand. Ford was also the first company to create a network of franchised dealers to sell its cars. By 1911, Ford began to expand internationally, opening factories throughout Europe. By 1919, half of all cars produced in the United States were Fords.

Will Durant founded General Motors in 1908. GM was founded as a holding company, or a company that buys and runs other companies. Durant used GM to buy existing vehicle manufacturers Buick, Cadillac, and Oldsmobile. It also purchased the Reliance Motor Company and Rapid Motor Vehicle Company, which eventually became the GMAC truck line of GM.

Chrysler started in 1923, when an automotive manufacturer called Maxwell-Chalmers went out of business. A man named Walter Chrysler took over the company. In 1925, he formed the Chrysler Company to produce his new line of automobiles.

The Ford Motor Company was the first automaker to build its cars using assembly line labor. Here, workers lower the body of a Ford Model T onto its chassis on an outdoor assembly line in Highland Park, Michigan, in 1914.

During the 1920s, Chrysler and General Motors began to take market share from Ford. Ford had concentrated on producing affordable cars with basic features. Chrysler and GM took a different path, introducing cars that were more luxurious. They also instituted financing that allowed customers to pay for cars in monthly installments, instead of having to pay for the entire cost of the car at one time. This allowed people to buy more expensive cars. To compete with these companies, Ford bought the Lincoln Motor Company in 1922. Lincoln provided Ford with a luxury auto line. In 1938, Ford added the modestly priced Mercury line of vehicles.

The Auto Industry in the Great Depression

The American auto industry grew quickly. By the 1930s, it had already become a major part of the national economy. However, the 1930s would ultimately be a time of great economic crisis for the United States.

In October 1929, the U.S. stock market crashed. Many banks that had extended money to people buying large amounts of stock failed. Unlike today, however, there was no Federal Deposit Insurance Corporation (FDIC). The FDIC protects the money that people have in banks. In its absence, many people lost most, or all, of their money.

What followed the stock market crash of October 1929 was an economic downturn that lasted a decade. This period is known as the Great Depression. The Great Depression changed the face of the auto industry.

Prior to 1930, there were a variety of small automobile manufacturers competing with Chrysler, Ford, and GM. But with about 25 percent of the population unemployed and credit difficult to obtain, auto sales declined. The reduction in auto sales during the 1930s spelled the end for many of the smaller car companies, leaving the Big Three in command of the industry.

At this time, things began changing among the Big Three. Until the 1930s, Ford had held the largest share of the automobile market. However, Chrysler and GM were quicker to respond to the new economic realities of the Great Depression. They began producing stylish, inexpensive cars. By doing so, Chrysler and GM hoped to draw purchasers away from Ford's simple, basic cars. Their strategies worked. By the end of the 1930s, GM had the largest market share of any U.S. auto manufacturer, followed by Chrysler and Ford.

The Rise of the United Auto Workers

The harsh working conditions and high unemployment that plagued the country during the 1930s angered many factory workers. Under President Franklin D.

Roosevelt, Congress passed the National Labor Relations Act in 1935. This act, among other things, protected the rights of workers to organize in labor unions. Representatives of these unions could engage in negotiations with company management to secure benefits and protections for workers. In 1941, Ford signed the first labor union agreement with the United Auto Workers (UAW). Today, the workers at Chrysler, Ford, and GM are all members of the UAW.

The Cult of the Automobile

The increased production of goods demanded by World War II (1939–1945) revived the flagging U.S. economy. The factories of Detroit turned to making arms and equipment for the war effort, rather than manufacturing automobiles. After the war ended, however, consumers' appetite for cars increased. A system of interstate highways was built across the United States, making travel faster and easier. Better highways also allowed people to live in suburbs, where there was no public transportation.

At the end of World War II, European countries were faced with rebuilding their infrastructure. At this time, America became the major supplier of manufactured goods to the world. This was very good for the U.S. economy. People began earning more money, and businesses flourished. Developers bought up land outside of

The National Interstate Highway System was developed in the 1950s to improve transportation throughout the United States. Today, the Interstate Highway System passes through all fifty states.

cities and built suburbs full of affordable housing for the expanding middle class and returning veterans.

For the first time, large numbers of people began living away from the downtown areas of cities where they worked. This meant they needed cars to get to and from work. This need fueled the demand for automobiles. American car companies churned out large, powerful, stylish cars for people to buy. These cars got poor mileage, but gas was inexpensive at the time.

Since American companies were doing so well, workers wanted their fair share. In the auto industry, unions demanded—and received—high wages. They also won generous pension arrangements and benefits, such as health care coverage that continued after their retirement.

When many of these benefits were first negotiated, the average life expectancy of people was much shorter than it is today. For example, in 1940, the average life expectancy in the United States was sixty-three years. Therefore, only a small proportion of workers reached retirement age and lived long enough to receive benefits for an extended period of time. Today, the average life expectancy in the United States is seventy-eight years. With the population living longer, providing benefits for life to retired workers has become a financial burden to auto companies. As larger numbers of workers retire, it costs the auto companies more and more to support them.

In the 1960s, while small, foreign-made cars were being imported into the United States, domestic companies produced cars that were large, powerful, and fast. They catered to consumers who wanted cars with powerful engines and stylish bodies. These high-performance cars could accelerate rapidly and had high top speeds. They were referred to as "muscle cars."

Mistakes and Mishaps

The glory days of the American automobile were about to end in a series of disastrous missteps. The focus was on producing big, stylish cars. The United States was a country with large highways and new, modern cities. In contrast, many cities in Europe were hundreds of years old and had narrow, winding streets. Large cars seemed to suit Americans.

Volkswagen, a German company, introduced the first successful small cars to America. In the 1960s, Volkswagen introduced a car called the Beetle to the U.S. market. Domestic car companies saw this tiny, no-frills car as a cheap form of transportation for young people who couldn't afford a bigger, better vehicle. American car companies did not think most customers would consider tiny cars like the Beetle as a serious alternative to large American cars.

Soon Japanese car companies, such as Datsun (now Nissan), Honda, and Toyota joined the race to supply small, inexpensive cars to the U.S. market. American car companies were used to dominating the U.S. auto market, and they did not believe these small, inexpensive imports presented a serious threat to their business. Management at domestic car companies still thought that Americans would never stop loving large, powerful cars. By the early 1970s, however, the reign of the large American car was threatened by the rise in gas prices.

Gas Prices on the Rise

At this time, American cars used enormous amounts of gasoline. Many only got seven to twelve miles (eleven to nineteen kilometers) per gallon. In 1973, the Middle Eastern oil cartel OPEC (Organization of Petroleum Exporting Countries) started cutting back on its production of oil. A cartel is an organization composed of manufacturers—in this case, oil manufacturers—who meet to set prices and output quotas, and to make other policy decisions. By cutting back on oil production, OPEC reduced the supply of oil available worldwide. This scarcity increased demand, which resulted in higher prices.

This 1965 photo, featuring a stylish couple posing with a Pontiac GTO convertible sports car, was typical for car advertisements of the time. Ads like this attempted to sell cars by tying them to people's self-image.

Oil is sold by the barrel and is refined into gasoline. Refineries in the United States purchase much of their oil from foreign producers, especially those in the Middle East. From 1950 to the early 1970s, the price of gasoline had remained below $1.50 per gallon (adjusted to present-day dollars). When OPEC began to raise prices, however, the price of gasoline rapidly increased to more than $2 per gallon. Prices remained high through 1985.

As the price of gasoline increased, consumers began to develop an interest in cars that got more miles per gallon. This meant buying smaller cars. American car companies began to face serious competition for the first time.

Foreign Competition

At the end of World War II, Japan focused on rebuilding its shattered economy. It did so by concentrating on manufacturing goods for civilian consumption. Japan developed a healthy automotive industry that produced high-quality, fuel-efficient, small cars.

Beginning in the 1970s, Japanese companies such as Toyota and Honda began exporting large numbers of cars to the United States. The United States also got cars from European manufacturers. German companies such

By the 1970s, automobiles from Japan began to flood the U.S. market. These cars impressed buyers with their reliability and low price and soon became very popular.

as BMW, Mercedes-Benz, and Volkswagen produced a number of cars popular with U.S. consumers, as did the Swedish companies Saab and Volvo. The automotive industry had become a global enterprise.

European companies began marketing their vehicles to the American public as high-performance, luxurious alternatives to American cars. Domestic car companies were not prepared for the popularity of small cars, and they were not used to dealing with such strong competition. When American car companies finally began producing some small cars to compete with their foreign competition, the vehicles they produced had reliability problems. They were also not as powerful as the foreign-made cars that they were competing with. As a result, many people came to see foreign cars as being better than American cars. Japanese car companies were making vehicles that were not only inexpensive, but which also had fewer mechanical problems. This hurt American car companies' sales.

A New Generation of Drivers

Things got even worse for U.S. car companies in the 1980s. By then, a younger generation of drivers had begun gravitating to sleek, foreign-made luxury cars instead of the Cadillacs and Lincolns that were favored by their parents. These younger consumers considered many formerly successful American brands to be old-fashioned. U.S. luxury brands like Cadillac stumbled for years trying to come up with a way to win younger, affluent car buyers back from foreign companies such as Mercedes-Benz, BMW, and Lexus.

In an attempt to capitalize on the appeal of foreign luxury cars, American car companies purchased or merged with foreign companies. For example, Ford bought the British luxury car manufacturer Jaguar and the Swedish car company Volvo. Chrysler was bought by German auto manufacturer Daimler-Benz in 1998, but it was later sold back to the private American investment firm Cerberus Capital Management. General Motors

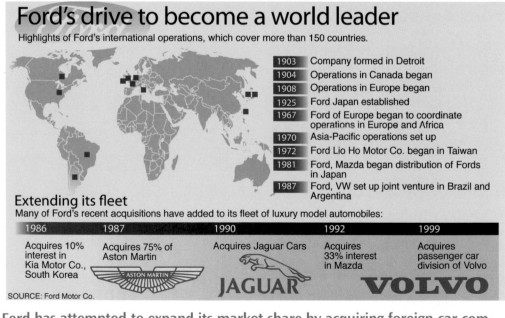

Ford has attempted to expand its market share by acquiring foreign car companies. This timeline shows Ford's international expansion over the years.

purchased the German car manufacturer Opel. Unfortunately, none of these efforts resulted in attracting significant numbers of customers away from BMW, Mercedes, Toyota, Honda, and other foreign brands.

Acquiring these companies caused an unforeseen problem for American car companies: Each company owned too many brands. After acquiring a foreign brand, an American car company took over the duties of manufacturing the car. However, these "new" car brands didn't just compete with rival car brands—they also competed with the other brands the company produced. In many ways, American auto companies were paying to compete with themselves as much as their actual competitors.

Finally, some of the foreign competitors proved to be more innovative than their American counterparts. For instance, foreign manufacturers led the field in developing hybrid vehicles, which used both gas and electrical power to dramatically improve gas mileage. When the economic downturn of 2008 to 2009 hit, American automotive companies saw their sales drop off.

The problems of the auto industry did not become critical until the economic crisis hit the United States—and the rest of the world. A number of issues relating to the crisis led to the collapse of Chrysler and GM. These included the need to refinance debt, a lack of consumer credit, and the inability of U.S. auto manufacturers to cut costs in order to be competitive with foreign manufacturers. The economic crisis brought the problems of automakers to a head.

The Economic Crisis

In 2008, the auto industry was hit with a devastating blow. In November, the U.S. stock market declined by 35 percent.

One of the major causes of the crash was speculation in the housing market, which drove up the price of houses. Because the mortgage market was lucrative, banks gave loans to more and more people, finally giving many mortgages to people who might not actually be able to pay them back. Eventually, people began to default on their loans, which means they were not able to pay them back. Banks foreclosed on these people's homes and put them up for sale. By selling the houses of those who defaulted on their loans, the banks hoped to make their money back.

However, as more and more houses came onto the market, housing prices dropped. The value of homes began to decrease. Many people found that they owed more money on their houses than the homes

Stock traders face the workday at the New York Stock Exchange on November 21, 2008. The market lost $1.3 trillion in value over the preceding two days.

themselves were actually worth. More and more of these homes went into foreclosure as well.

The value of the homes that the banks owned decreased. This meant the value of the assets held by the banks also decreased. The banks had to write off millions of dollars in bad loans, which means they had to subtract them from their profits. Faced with this reduction in their assets, and afraid that the people they lent money to would default on the loans, the banks stopped providing credit.

The shaky state of the major financial institutions and the potential lack of credit sparked fear among investors. These investors were afraid that many companies, unable to borrow cash for operations, would inevitably fail. Investors sold vast amounts of stock. This resulted in the stock market crash of 2008.

People saw the value of their investments and their retirement accounts plummet. Many people had relied on their homes as collateral for a type of loan called a home equity loan. Home equity loans allow homeowners to borrow against the value of their home. As the value of houses fell, people's available credit also fell. Many businesses, unable to borrow money for operations, failed. People began to be laid off.

Many other companies, including very large ones, saw there would be less demand for their products and services. This was because of the high unemployment in the wake of the crisis and because companies couldn't borrow money to buy things. Therefore, they also began to lay off workers and cut back on production. Millions of people lost their homes to foreclosure, and millions more lost their jobs. By August 2009, unemployment reached 9.7 percent, or 14.9 million U.S. citizens.

One major result of the turmoil in the finance industry was that individual consumers couldn't get loans for large purchases, such as a car. Even those consumers who still had cash or adequate credit were afraid to make large purchases, preferring to save their money in case they were laid off. Auto sales declined by more than 70 percent.

The Effect of the Crisis on the Auto Manufacturers

The radical slump in auto sales meant that automakers' earnings decreased. Soon their income did not cover their business expenses. It also made it difficult for them to borrow money to keep operating. Banks were reluctant to lend money to anybody, and an automaker whose sales had dropped 70 percent was a risky borrower.

At the time of the crash, Ford had an emergency fund of $10 billion that it had put aside. GM and Chrysler, however, already had very high levels of debt. They knew that they would not be able to refinance their debt because of the banking crisis. The automakers did not have the money to pay their debts, and there was no way they could borrow more.

To make matters worse, the automakers were tied into contracts with union workers and with an enormous network of dealers. The auto companies had no way to change those contractual agreements. The chief executive officers of the Big Three went to Washington, D.C., to appeal for help.

In November 2009, approximately sixteen million U.S. citizens were out of work. That month, the unemployment rate reached 10.2 percent, the highest it had been in over twenty-five years. Because of the financial crisis, many people were reluctant to make large purchases.

Bailout or Bust?

In October 2008, the Emergency Economic Stabilization Act of 2008 was passed by Congress and signed into law by President George W. Bush. The act set up the Troubled Asset Relief Program (TARP). TARP was authorized to spend up to $700 billion to make loans to financial institutions. These financial institutions were so large that, if they failed, they could affect the entire U.S. economy.

Faced with the drastic decline in sales, auto manufacturers would need assistance to keep from collapsing. In November 2008, the chief executive officers of Ford, GM, and Chrysler went to Washington, D.C., to appeal to the U.S. government for loans from the TARP funds in order to keep operating. They were told to return with detailed plans on how they would reorganize their businesses so that lawmakers could see how the companies would remain operational if they received TARP funds.

In December 2008, the Bush administration made $17.4 billion in loans available to the auto manufacturers. Ford did not borrow money from the federal government, but GM and Chrysler did. The fact that the government provided funds to the automakers caused a great controversy. Those in favor of providing the funds believed the auto industry was such a large segment of the economy that letting the automakers go out of business would have devastating results. The huge job losses that would follow the collapse of the automakers would be devastating to the economy. In addition, suppliers to the automakers would also go bankrupt, further increasing unemployment.

Many of those opposed to bailing out the industry believed the funds provided would not be sufficient to keep the auto manufacturers afloat. If this proved to be

On October 3, 2008, President George W. Bush signed the Emergency Economic Stabilization Act of 2008 into law. Among other things, this act bailed out many of the United States' banks. Two months later, the government loaned $17.4 billion to the U.S. auto industry.

the case, the government would simply be throwing tax-payers' money away.

Others were opposed to loaning the automakers money because they believed that, in a free-market economy, "bad" companies should be allowed to fail. If this happened, they would be replaced by "good" companies.

There was still another issue, one of national pride. The companies that would rise up to replace the failed U.S. auto companies would likely be Japanese companies such as Toyota and Honda. They would almost certainly not be American companies. Even though foreign car companies maintained factories in the United States and employed American workers, many people didn't want to see the American auto industry die.

Coping with the Crisis

In December 2008, the U.S. Treasury authorized the distribution of loans from the TARP program to U.S. automakers. Loans worth $13.4 billion were given to GM, and $4 billion worth were given to Chrysler. Ford did not take the loans, although it arranged for a line of credit with the Treasury Department that it could draw on later if it needed to. As part of the auto industry bailout, the Obama administration required U.S. automakers to focus on making more eco-friendly, fuel-efficient cars.

In December, the U.S. Treasury invested $5 billion in GMAC, the finance arm of General Motors. The Treasury provided $1 billion in loans to GM to reorganize GMAC as a separate commercial bank. Since banks were reluctant to lend money to consumers, the Treasury extended $1.5 billion in financing to Chrysler in January 2009 for the purpose of setting up a finance unit. This would allow the company to provide credit to people who needed loans to purchase cars.

Restructuring

In February 2009, President Barack Obama created a task force to oversee the restructuring of American auto manufacturers. Members from departments of the federal government involved with the automotive industry made up this task force. It included representatives from the Departments of Transportation, Energy, Labor, Commerce, and the Treasury. It also included representatives from the president's Council of Economic Advisers, the White House Office of Energy and Climate Change Policy, and the National Economic Council.

On April 30, 2009, President Barack Obama announced the members of his auto task force at the White House. The task force was assembled to help stabilize the U.S. auto industry.

Treasury Secretary Timothy Geithner and the director of the National Economic Council, Larry Summers, were put in charge of the task force. One of the task force's key activities was to review the reorganization plans submitted for Chrysler and GM. Ron Bloom, an expert on restructuring industrial companies, was appointed special adviser to the Treasury in regard to the reorganization of the automakers. Bloom was promptly dubbed the "Car Czar" by the mass media.

Banks weren't the only companies wary of doing business with ailing auto manufacturers. Suppliers of parts and other materials were concerned that the automakers might fail and they would not be paid for their goods. In response to the need to keep necessary parts flowing to the automakers, the U.S. Treasury implemented the $5 billion Auto Supplier Support Program in March 2009. Under the program, the Treasury guaranteed payment for receivables (money owed) to qualified suppliers by the automakers. The program then allowed those suppliers to draw funds from the Treasury against outstanding invoices.

Giving loans to the automakers would allow them to continue operating for several months. During this time, they were to restructure their operations. It was believed that, if the companies could change certain elements of their operations, they would be able to lower their costs enough to survive.

The restructuring required the automakers to negotiate changes with the UAW regarding the salaries they paid their workers. American autoworkers received a salary that was generally higher than those paid to employees of foreign auto companies. The restructuring also required the union to agree to reductions in benefits for workers and retirees. For example, they were asked to eliminate the jobs bank, which pays workers most of their salary after they've been laid off. In addition, the companies would need to get bondholders to agree to reduced interest payments. The large interest payments that auto companies had to make to bondholders were putting a strain on the cash-strapped automotive industry.

Reinventing the Automakers

Not all of the automakers were in the same financial state at this time. In addition, each of them had different lines of vehicles and types of ownership. Therefore, each company took a different approach to restructuring.

Ford

When the financial crisis struck the United States, Ford was in a somewhat better position to weather the disaster than the other U.S. automakers. There are a couple of reasons for this. Ford had been working for some time to restructure its operations and reduce its costs. It had already improved its financial situation by renegotiating a number of contractual arrangements with its union employees.

Ford had also been building an emergency reserve fund in which it had amassed around $10 billion at the time of the financial collapse. While this amount was not enough to see the company through an extended downturn, it was enough of a cushion to allow Ford to further reorganize its operations without having to resort to bankruptcy. Ford was also a forward-thinking company: It had already developed the Ford Fusion, a hybrid car.

Chrysler

Seventy-three percent of Chrysler's production and 74 percent of its workforce are in the United States. It purchases 78 percent of its material from U.S. suppliers. At the time of the economic crisis, Chrysler was partially owned by

The development of next-generation, environmentally friendly, high-mileage vehicles is key to the survival of U.S. automakers. One such vehicle is the Ford Fusion, a gas/electric hybrid.

the investment firm Cerberus Capital Management. Other investment firms owned large amounts of Chrysler's stock.

On April 30, 2009, President Obama's auto task force tried to broker an arrangement whereby all stockholders and bondholders in the firm could reach an agreement that would allow the firm to continue functioning. However, the terms of the plan would have caused significant financial losses for stockholders and bond- holders. As a result, the government could not get all of the investment firms to agree to the plan.

Chrysler could not avoid bankruptcy. The govern- ment assisted Chrysler to design a reorganization plan that would allow the company to go through the bank- ruptcy process rapidly. As part of the restructuring, Italian auto manufacturer Fiat, which already had a stake in Chrysler, purchased a significant share of the company. Fiat wished to gain a presence in the U.S. car market.

Under the terms of Chrysler's bankruptcy plan, the UAW's retirement fund became the biggest shareholder in the reorganized company. The U.S. government and Fiat were smaller shareholders. The government also made a line of credit available to Chrysler so that it could borrow money.

Chrysler's April 30, 2009, bankruptcy was the first for a U.S. automaker since 1933, when the carmaker

Studebaker went into bankruptcy. The reason for expediting the bankruptcy process was that President Obama wished to preserve jobs for American workers. This meant Chrysler had to remain a viable company. However, it was running through $100 million per day while its manufacturing plants were idle. Therefore, getting the company reorganized and back in business as soon as possible was key to its survival.

The bankruptcy proceeding was announced on April 30, 2009, and the company completed the proceedings in June 2009. Under the terms of the final agreement, the UAW retirement trust owned 55 percent of the company, Fiat owned a 20 percent share that could potentially grow to 35 percent under the agreement, and the U.S. and Canadian governments owned the remaining shares. In this case, the Canadian government participated because Chrysler has factories in Canada, and the Canadian government wished to protect its workers' jobs as well.

Chrysler has traditionally been dependent on sales of its large vehicles, such as Jeeps, trucks, and vans. Fiat's line of small cars could provide Chrysler with entry into that market—and help it avoid the stigma associated with American-made small cars. However, the Fiat designs may first have to be adjusted to meet U.S. environmental emission standards. Therefore, it could be a while before Fiats appear at Chrysler dealerships.

General Motors

The U.S. government wanted to see major changes in the structure and policies of the auto industry in return for providing funding. As part of these changes, the Obama administration asked GM's chief executive officer, Richard Wagoner Jr., to resign. They believed that Wagoner had not made the kinds of changes necessary for GM to avoid bankruptcy.

Under Wagoner's control, GM had gone from a 28 percent U.S. market share in 2000 to a 20 percent market share in 2008. In addition, a deal with Italian automaker Fiat that cost GM $4.5 billion, and the ill-conceived purchase of the Hummer brand, were seen as contributing factors to the company's woes. Wagoner was replaced by GM Chief Operating Officer Frederick Henderson. On December 1, 2009, Henderson resigned and Ed Whitacre became acting CEO until a new one could be found.

Ultimately, the money provided by the government was not sufficient to keep GM in business. At the same time, a drawn-out bankruptcy would result in all the negative effects of vast unemployment discussed earlier. Therefore, the Obama administration put together a plan for a streamlined bankruptcy that would allow GM to complete the process in a matter of months, restructure, and then resume operations.

Rick Wagoner stepped down as chairman and CEO of General Motors on March 30, 2009. The U.S. government requested that Wagoner resign as part of its agreement to help restructure GM.

Bankruptcy would essentially eliminate all of GM's existing contracts with the UAW and erase its debt obligations. Freed of debt and restructured, the company would have a chance to reinvent itself. One hitch in this plan was the company's bondholders. Under U.S. bankruptcy laws, bondholders have the right to be paid out of a company's assets. If the bondholders took the company's assets, it wouldn't be able to continue operating. Therefore, the Obama administration worked hard to get bondholders to accept stock in the company in lieu of the assets that they were entitled to.

The initial plan allocated 39 percent of the stock in the restructured GM to the UAW, 50 percent to the U.S. government, and 10 percent to the bondholders. The details of the plan were subsequently altered, but the concept remained the same. All of the company's key players would get a stake in the new company. By getting agreement in advance from all of the interested parties, the company would be able to go through the bankruptcy process rapidly. GM's bankruptcy was the largest that had ever occurred in the United States.

Cash for Clunkers

On June 19, 2009, Congress passed the Automotive Stimulus bill, popularly dubbed Cash for Clunkers. The bill provided a tax credit of $4,500 for people who traded an old car in for a newer, more fuel-efficient one. The idea was to both stimulate auto sales and get people to trade in their old, non-fuel-efficient vehicles for cars that were more environmentally friendly.

The government's Cash for Clunkers program proved to be very successful. Ultimately, $3 billion was provided to car buyers.

The Cash for Clunkers program successfully increased auto sales, and the government gave out $2.9 billion in rebates. Approximately seven hundred thousand new cars were sold under the program, which provided much-needed cash for the automakers. Ford and GM boosted production at their factories to meet the demand for vehicles under the program. However, it remains to be seen how the car companies fare now that the program is over. Slow sales and tight credit for those trying to purchase vehicles remain major issues.

5 The Road Ahead

On June 2, 2009, Chrysler emerged from bank-ruptcy proceedings. GM did the same on July 10, 2009. The United States was still in the middle of a recession, however, so all of the Big Three automakers still faced a long hard road ahead. Many changes lie ahead for them. Chrysler, Ford, and GM are all taking steps to become more competitive in terms of corporate structure and vehicles offered.

The New General Motors

The restructured GM will look quite different from the old GM. For one thing, it will have fewer lines of cars. The Pontiac brand is being eliminated, and the company is selling its Hummer, Saab, and Saturn lines. GM will keep Buick, Cadillac, Chevrolet, and GMAC. This means the company has one economy, midrange, and luxury car line, as well as a truck line, instead of multiple brands all competing with each other. In addition, the reduction in car lines will allow it to eliminate up to 1,600 dealers.

In February 2009, GM developed a plan designed to return it to profitability in two years. The plan focused on streamlining operations, as well as reducing brands, dealerships, and manufacturing facilities. The company planned to focus on four brands: Buick, Cadillac, Chevrolet, and GMAC (trucks). As part of this plan, it made the commitment that twenty-two of twenty-four new vehicles scheduled to be introduced between 2009

In 2005, GM became the largest overseas automaker in China. U.S. automakers hope that they will be able to sell cars to the large, new middle class that is growing in emerging markets like China.

and 2014 would be highly fuel-efficient, or hybrids. It also planned to restructure its arrangements with the UAW. This would allow the company to get labor costs down to a level that would be competitive with those of foreign auto manufacturers operating in the United States.

GM does a great deal of business and manufacturing overseas. Therefore, it's also working with governments in Canada, Europe, and the Asia-Pacific region to sustain operations in those areas. GM tried to sell its German Opel unit. However, it was forced to drop

To be successful, alternative energy cars must be attractive and powerful, as well as efficient. This Chrysler Dodge EV electric sports car, displayed at a 2008 auto show, shows that environmentally friendly cars can also be fun.

these plans because of objections by European regulators and unions, which formed job loses.

GM is also reaching out directly to the public. The company has launched an ad campaign designed to convince consumers that, as it emerges from bankruptcy, it is reinventing itself. In addition to traditional media like television, the company is reaching out to consumers through social networking sites such as Twitter and Facebook. GM also has started a pilot program with the auction Web site eBay to sell cars online, and it is currently working on an electric car called the Chevy Volt.

The New Chrysler

Chrysler is reducing its manufacturing capacity by 30 percent. It is eliminating twelve shifts, laying off thirty-two thousand workers, and discontinuing four models. Chrysler is also selling $700 million of its assets and reducing how many dealers it has. Finally, the company has obtained concessions from the UAW that put compensation for union workers at Chrysler on par with those of foreign automakers operating in the United States.

Chrysler plans to improve both the overall quality and fuel economy of its cars. In 2010, it will introduce a new engine, the Phoenix V-6. The company expects that the Phoenix V-6 will provide a 6 to 8 percent improvement in fuel efficiency. Chrysler's merger with Fiat should also help it improve fuel efficiency, as the company will be able to utilize Fiat's smaller, more fuel-efficient engines, and other energy-saving technologies. Access to these technologies could reduce the cost of redesign for Chrysler. It also plans to introduce a hybrid version of its bestselling vehicle, the Dodge Ram truck. In addition, Chrysler intends to release its first electric-drive vehicle in 2010. It plans to produce more electric-drive vehicles in the future.

Chrysler is also focusing on improving the quality of its vehicles. The company has appointed a chief customer officer. The chief customer officer will oversee the improvement of quality in Chrysler vehicles and will also improve the perception of quality on the part of car buyers. To support these efforts, Chrysler has formed customer satisfaction teams. These teams will act as problem-solvers for new vehicles as they are being developed and launched. Chrysler plans to launch revised versions of four of its most successful lines: Dodge Charger, Dodge Durango, Chrysler 300, and Jeep Grand Cherokee.

The New Ford

Ford's image as a well-managed car company was enhanced by the fact that it did not go bankrupt along with Chrysler and GM. In addition, Ford was able to take advantage of uncertainty about the future of Chrysler and GM while those companies were undergoing bankruptcy.

Beyond this, the improved quality of Ford cars, and the appeal of new models such as the Ford Fusion hybrid, helped the company's reputation. Consumer confidence in Ford and its products was high. As a result, in the fall of 2009, Ford was able to reduce the incentives it offered to customers. Going forward, this will provide the company with lower costs and higher profit margins.

In an effort to reduce its corporate debt by 40 percent, Ford developed a plan to give creditors stock in lieu of cash payments. It also negotiated arrangements with the UAW in which the union would, for half of the payments the company put into its employee health care fund, accept stock instead of cash. Ford opened a line of credit with the Treasury Department that it could draw on if needed, but the company committed to a self-financed recovery.

Ford's approach to dealing with the financial crisis has improved the way the company is viewed by consumers in comparison to GM and Chrysler. Like its competitors, Ford is concentrating on fuel-efficient cars to win consumer and government support. The Ford Fusion hybrid has recently come to market. Ford will be releasing a new version of its successful midsized car, the Ford Taurus. The redesigned version will feature the new EcoBoost

Newly built Ford EcoBoost engines move down the assembly line at a manufacturing plant in May 2009 in Brook Park, Ohio. New, energy-efficient technologies are key to the future of U.S. automakers.

engine. Ford will be introducing the Fiesta subcompact in 2010. In 2011, the company plans to introduce an electric car. In 2012, it is going to put a plug-in car on the market.

Going Green

The Obama administration has repeatedly emphasized the need for U.S. automakers to focus on green technology. It is believed that cars using green technology will likely be in demand in the future. As part of the process of restructuring, the administration is requiring the automakers to produce more fuel-efficient vehicles. The administration's idea is that consumers who want to

In August 2009, General Motors CEO and President Fritz Henderson announced that the new Chevy Volt extended range vehicle, shown here, would get an estimated 230 miles (370 kilometers) per gallon.

avoid high gas prices will buy these vehicles. At the same time, such cars would, in theory, be better for the environment. Both Chrysler and GM may receive several billion dollars from the U.S. Department of Energy to assist them with developing greener cars.

The Challenges Ahead

The crisis in the automotive industry has presented U.S. car companies with the opportunity to remake themselves. However, the question remains: Will they be able to successfully win back the car-buying public and thus survive and prosper?

One of the greatest obstacles that U.S. automakers have to overcome is the perception that the cars they make are inferior to those made by their foreign competitors. According to a recent survey by J. D. Power and Associates, concern about reliability is one of the key reasons why consumers avoid certain car brands. According to a May 2009 *BusinessWeek* special report, 51 percent of those in Generation Y (people born from the late 1970s through the 1990s) would consider buying a Toyota, whereas only a little more than 30 percent would consider a Ford or GM car. Only 10 percent would consider purchasing a Chrysler.

The bottom line is that American automakers not only need to make different cars, but they also need to make better cars. Ford has already made great strides in this area. A survey conducted by the RDA Group, a market research firm, compared customer satisfaction with the newest models of Ford and other automotive manufacturers. The survey found that the newest Ford, Mercury, and Lincoln vehicles had slightly fewer problems than those made by Toyota and Honda. In addition, both Ford and Toyota had an 80 percent customer satisfaction rating.

However, even if American automakers produce more reliable cars, it may not be easy for them to overcome long-held perceptions that American-made cars are less reliable than Japanese cars. Therefore, the future success of U.S. automakers may rest on their ability to convince the public that the cars they are producing are well made and reliable. This point was brought home by the results of the Cash for Clunkers program. After trading in their old cars, many Americans purchased foreign cars.

A second issue relates to the new types of vehicles the car companies are tying their future to. The U.S. government under President Obama has applied significant pressure on the American auto manufacturers to produce primarily fuel-efficient, ecologically sound vehicles. There is no doubt that when gas prices briefly went higher than $4 per gallon in 2008, consumers demonstrated an interest in such vehicles. However, since that time, the cost of gas has dropped significantly. It remains to be seen if Americans, who have traditionally gravitated toward large vehicles, will be attracted to smaller automobiles. Until the economy and credit lending recover, and vehicle sales pick up, the answer to this question remains unknown.

Glossary

accelerate To increase in speed.

allocate To set something apart for a specific purpose.

asset An item of value.

bailout Financial assistance that a company receives to keep it from collapsing.

bankruptcy A legal proceeding in which a company that cannot meet its financial obligations is reorganized or dissolved.

bond A financial instrument that guarantees regular interest payments to the bondholder.

cartel A group of businesses that jointly sets pricing and policies for an industry.

collateral Something of value that a lender can take possession of if a loan is not repaid.

default To not repay a loan.

depression An economic downturn that is worse than a recession.

expedite To speed up the process of doing something.

foreclosure The act of a bank taking over a property that it provided a loan for.

fuel-efficient Using less fuel to operate.

home equity loan A loan for which a person's house is used as collateral.

infrastructure Facilities necessary for a community to function, such as roads, bridges, and buildings.

line of credit Credit provided by a bank that the borrower can draw on as needed.

lucrative Valuable, or worth money.

mortgage A loan provided to pay for a piece of property.

pension A fixed amount of money paid to retired workers on a regular schedule, or in a lump sum.

pilot program A small-scale effort designed to test a project before expanding it on a larger scale.

recession A downturn in the economy; a period in which the overall value of the goods and services produced by a country shrinks.

refinery A facility that processes oil into gasoline.

revenue Money received as income.

trust A legal setup in which money is held for the benefit of certain persons.

union A group of workers who form an organization to bargain with management.

write off Take as a loss against profits.

For More Information

AACA Antique Auto Museum at Hershey
1161 Museum Drive
Hershey, PA 17033
(717) 466-7100
Web site: http://www.aacamuseum.org
This museum features eight decades of automobiles and other vehicles, as well as memorabilia. The museum holds workshops designed to educate people about the impact automobiles have had on American culture.

General Motors
P.O. Box 33170
Detroit, MI 48232
Web site: http://www.gm.com
A Big Three automaker, GM is currently undergoing major changes.

Henry Ford Museum
20900 Oakwood Boulevard
Dearborn, MI 48124
(313) 892-5029
Web site: http://www.thehenryford.org
This museum features exhibits on the automobile, as well as a Ford factory tour.

United Auto Workers
Solidarity House
8000 East Jefferson Avenue
Detroit, MI 48214
(313) 926-5000
Web site: http://www.uaw.org
This is the headquarters of the union to which all U.S. autoworkers belong.

U.S. Department of the Treasury
1500 Pennsylvania Avenue SW
Washington, DC 20220
(202) 622-2000
Web site: http://www.ustreas.gov
The Department of the Treasury is involved in reorganizing the auto companies and providing them with financing.

Web Sites

Due to the changing nature of Internet links, Rosen Publishing has developed an online list of Web sites related to the subject of this book. This site is updated regularly. Please use this link to access the list:

http://www.rosenlinks.com/itn/auto

For Further Reading

Cheetham, Craig. *The Encyclopedia of Classic Cars: From 1890 to the Present Day.* Charlotte, NC: Thunder Bay Press, 2007.

Clifford, Tim. *Our Economy in Action.* Vero Beach, FL: Rourke Publishing, 2008.

Collins, Tom. *The Legendary Model T.* Iola, WI: Krause Publishing, 2007.

Consumer Guide Editors. *Encyclopedia of American Cars.* Lincolnwood, IL: Consumer Guide, 2006.

Davis, Michael W. B. *Chrysler Heritage: A Photographic History.* Chicago, IL: Arcadia Publishing, 2001.

Davis, Michael W. B. *Detroit's Wartime Industry.* Chicago, IL: Arcadia Publishing, 2007.

Davis, Michael W. B. *Ford Dynasty: A Photographic History.* Chicago, IL: Arcadia Publishing, 2002.

Davis, Michael W. B. *General Motors: A Photographic History.* Chicago, IL: Arcadia Publishing, 1999.

Flynn, Sean Masaki. *Economics for Dummies.* Hoboken, NJ: Wiley Publishing, 2005.

Ford, Henry. *My Life and Work: An Autobiography of Henry Ford.* New York, NY: Classic House Books, 2009.

Gitlin, Marty. *The 1929 Stock Market Crash.* Edina, MN: Abdo Publishing, 2008

Glancey, Jonathan. *The Car: A History of the Automobile.* London, England: Carlton Books, 2008.

Heitmann, John. *The Automobile and American Life.* Jefferson, NC: McFarland, 2009.

Hovey, Craig, and Gregory Rehmke. *The Complete Idiot's Guide to Global Economics.* New York, NY: Penguin, 2008.

Hunnicutt, Susan C. *What Is the Future of the U.S. Economy?* Chicago, IL: Greenhaven Press, 2008.

Lang, Brenda. *The Stock Market Crash of 1929: The End of Prosperity.* New York, NY: Chelsea House, 2007.

Langworth, Richard M. *GM 100 Years.* Lincolnwood, IL: Consumer Guide, 2008.

Lyons, Daniel. *Cars of the Sensational '60s.* Iola, WI: Krause Publications, 2006.

Skurzynski, Gloria. *Sweat and Blood: A History of U.S. Labor Unions.* Minneapolis, MN: Twenty-First Century Books, 2008.

Wagner, Viqi. *Labor Unions.* Chicago, IL: Greenhaven Press, 2007.

Weber, Lou, ed. *American Cars of the 1950s.* Lincolnwood, IL: Consumer Guide, 2005.

Bibliography

Associated Press. "Bankrupt GM Changes Its Tone with Consumers." MSNBC.com, June 2, 2009. Retrieved August 5, 2009 (http://www.msnbc.msn.com/id/31071605).

Bureau of Labor Statistics. "Employment Situation Summary." U.S. Department of Labor. September 4, 2009. Retrieved September 4, 2009 (http://www.bls.gov/news.release/empsit.nr0.htm).

BusinessWeek. "Special Report: Auto Bailout: Crunch Time for Detroit." March 25, 2009. Retrieved August 26, 2009 (http://www.businessweek.com/bwdaily/dnflash/special_reports/20090325auto_bailout.htm).

Chrysler. "Chrysler Restructuring Plan for Long-Term Viability." FinancialStability.gov. February 17, 2009. Retrieved August 15, 2009 (http://www.financialstability.gov/docs/AIFP/ChryslerRestructuringPlanSummary.pdf).

CNN Money. "Ford's Fuel-Efficient Future." CNN.com, May 6, 2009. Retrieved August 16, 2009 (http://money.cnn.com/galleries/2009/autos/0904/gallery.ford_fuel_efficient/index.html).

CNN Money. "Panel to Advise President on Carmakers." CNN.com, February 16, 2009. Retrieved August 20,

2009 (http://money.cnn.com/2009/02/16/news/compa-nies/obama_auto_task_force/index.htm).

Currie, Antony. "Ford Raises Restructuring Bar." *Fortune*, March 5, 2009. Retrieved August 16, 2009 (http://money.cnn.com/2009/03/05/news/companies/break-ing_views.breakingviews/index.htm).

de la Merced, Michael J., and Michelle Maynard. "Fiat Deal with Chrysler Seals Swift 42-Day Overhaul." *New York Times*, June 10, 2009. Retrieved August 2, 2009 (http://www.nytimes.com/2009/06/11/business/global/11chrysler.html).

Galbraith, John Kenneth. *The Great Crash: 1929*. Boston, MA: Houghton-Mifflin, 1997.

General Motors. "Restructuring Plan 2009–2014." February 17, 2009. Retrieved August 15, 2009 (http://graphics8.nytimes.com/packages/pdf/busi-ness/20090217GMRestructuringPlan.pdf).

J. D. Power & Associates. "Vehicle Price and Gas Mileage Play Increasingly Important Roles in Vehicle Consideration." November 25, 2008. Retrieved August 1, 2009 (http://www.jdpower.com/corporate/news/releases/pressrelease.aspx?ID=2008254).

Mahler, Jonathan. "G.M., Detroit, and the Fall of the Black Middle Class." *New York Times* Magazine, June 28, 2009, pp. 30–47.

Rutenberg, Jim, and Bill Vlasic. "Chrysler Files to Receive Bankruptcy Protection." *New York Times*, April 30, 2009. Retrieved August 2, 2009 (http://www.nytimes.com/2009/05/01/business/01auto.html).

UPI. "Survey: Ford Tops Toyota's New Car Quality." UPI.com, July 21, 2009. Retrieved August 5, 2009 (http://www.upi.com/Business_News/2009/07/21/Survey-Ford-tops-Toyotas-new-car-quality/UPI-61891248192944). (http://www.commerce.wa.gov/energy/archive/Indicators99/Indicator24.htm).

U.S. News & World Report. "American Dream and Middle Class in Jeopardy." October 9, 2008. Retrieved August 14, 2009 (http://www.usnews.com/articles/science/culture/2008/10/09/american-dream-and-middle-class-in-jeopardy.html).

Washington State Department of Commerce. "Washington's Energy Indicators: Energy Price Trends—U.S. Gasoline Prices Since 1950." Retrieved August 15, 2009 (http://www.commerce.wa.gov/energy/archive/Indicators99/Indicator24.htm).

Index

About the Author

Jeri Freedman has a B.A. from Harvard University. For fifteen years she worked for high-technology companies, where her duties included investor relations. She is the author of more than thirty young adult nonfiction books, including *Get Smart with Your Money: First Bank Account and First Investments Smarts* and *In the News: The U.S. Economic Crisis.*

Photo Credits

Cover (top left), p. 5 Scott Olson/Getty Image; cover (top right) Stan Honda/AFP/Getty Images; cover (bottom) Spencer Platt/Getty Images; pp. 4, 10, 44, 51 Bill Pugliano/Getty Images; pp. 9, 42, 43, 46, 50 © AP Images; p. 11 Sipa Press/Newscom; pp. 13, 14, 21 Hulton Archive/Getty Images; p. 18 Harold M. Lambert/Hulton Archive/Getty Images; p. 22 Peter Jordan/Time & Life Pictures/Getty Images; p. 24 KRT/Newscom; pp. 26, 30 Justin Sullivan/Getty Images; p. 27 Mario Tama/Getty Images; p. 32 Brendan Smialowski/Getty Images; pp. 34, 38 Gabirel Bouys/AFP/Getty Images; p. 35 Chip Somodevilla/Getty Images; p. 45 Newscom.

Designer: Tom Forget; Photo Researcher: Peter Tomlinson